EYEWITNESS TO HISTORY

LEONARDO DA VINCI

in his own words

Gareth Stevens
PUBLISHING

By
Caroline
Kennon

Please visit our website, www.garethstevens.com. For a free color catalog of all our high-quality books, call toll free 1-800-542-2595 or fax 1-877-542-2596.

Library of Congress Cataloging-in-Publication Data

Kennon, Caroline, author.
 Leonardo da Vinci in his own words / Caroline Kennon.
     pages cm. — (Eyewitness to history)
 Includes index.
 ISBN 978-1-4824-4074-4 (pbk.)
 ISBN 978-1-4824-4075-1 (6 pack)
 ISBN 978-1-4824-4076-8 (library binding)
 1. Leonardo, da Vinci, 1452-1519—Juvenile literature. 2. Artists—Italy—Biography—Juvenile literature. 3. Scientists—Italy—Biography—Juvenile literature. I. Title.
 N6923.L33 K46
 709.2—dc23

                                    2015032046

First Edition

Published in 2016 by
Gareth Stevens Publishing
111 East 14th Street, Suite 349
New York, NY 10003

Designer: Katelyn E. Reynolds
Editor: Therese Shea

Photo credits: Cover, p. 1 (Leonardo da Vinci) Hulton Archive/Getty Images; cover, pp. 1 (background image), 16–17 Quibik/Wikipedia.org; cover, p. 1 (logo quill icon) Seamartini Graphics Media/Shutterstock.com; cover, p. 1 (logo stamp) YasnaTen/ Shutterstock.com; cover, p. 1 (color grunge frame) DmitryPrudnichenko/Shutterstock.com; cover, pp. 1–32 (paper background) Nella/Shutterstock.com; cover, pp. 1–32 (decorative elements) Ozerina Anna/Shutterstock.com; pp. 1–32 (wood texture) Reinhold Leitner/ Shutterstock.com; pp. 1–32 (open book background) Elena Schweitzer/Shutterstock.com; pp. 1–32 (bookmark) Robert Adrian Hillman/Shutterstock.com; p. 5 Leemage/Universal Images Group/Getty Images; pp. 6–7 Gina Martin/National Geographic/Getty Images; pp. 9 (top), 12 Amandajm/Wikipedia.org; p. 9 (bottom) Amada44/Wikipedia.org; pp. 10, 13, 21, 25 Dcoetzee/Wikipedia.org; p. 11 Sailko/Wikipedia.org; p. 15 (left) Botaurus/ Wikipedia.org; p. 15 (right) Oursana/Wikipedia.org; p. 19 Arianna/Wikipedia.org; p. 23 DcoetzeeBot/Wikipedia.org; p. 27 World Imaging/Wikipedia.org; p. 28 Russell Mountford/ Lonely Planet Images/Getty Images.

Printed in the United States of America

CPSIA compliance information: Batch #CW16GS: For further information contact Gareth Stevens, New York, New York at 1-800-542-2595.

CONTENTS

*Words in the glossary appear in **bold** type the first time they are used in the text.*

The RENAISSANCE *Man*

Leonardo da Vinci is most famous for his paintings, but he's also respected for many other accomplishments. He was an artist, a musician, an **architect**, a scientist, and a writer. He became all these despite a lack of formal education. He never attended a university—or any school at all. And yet, today, he's recognized and celebrated for his intelligence.

Because Leonardo never had a higher education, he faced certain obstacles and **prejudices**: *"They will say that I, having no literary skill, cannot properly express that which I desire [to express]; but they do not know that my subjects are to be dealt with by experience rather than by words."* He taught himself about many fields of art and science through both study and experience.

This is thought to be a portrait that Leonardo created of himself at the end of his life. It was done in red chalk.

RENAISSANCE MAN

Leonardo is perhaps the most famous example of a "Renaissance man." The Renaissance was a period of history that began in the 14th century. The word "renaissance" comes from a French word that means "rebirth." This was a time of renewed interest in art, literature, and science. A Renaissance man is one who's interested and skilled in several areas of learning, especially art, science, and math. Another term for a Renaissance man is "polymath," from a Greek word meaning "very learned."

YOUNG *Leonardo*

Leonardo was born near Vinci in modern-day Italy on April 15, 1452. His mother was a peasant or a servant, and his father was a **notary** and a landlord. They weren't permitted to marry because of their different backgrounds. By the time Leonardo was 5, he was living with his grandfather.

Young Leonardo spent a lot of time with his uncle Francesco, who taught him how to make oil from olives. This would be important, for paint was made much the same way olive oil was. Leonardo later wrote, *"Those who are in love with practice without knowledge are like the sailor who gets into a ship without **rudder** or compass and who never can be certain [where] he is going."* Despite his lack of schooling, Leonardo was gaining practical knowledge every day.

This is what the olive groves look like in Vinci today. Leonardo would later sketch an olive press, perhaps a memory from his time with his uncle.

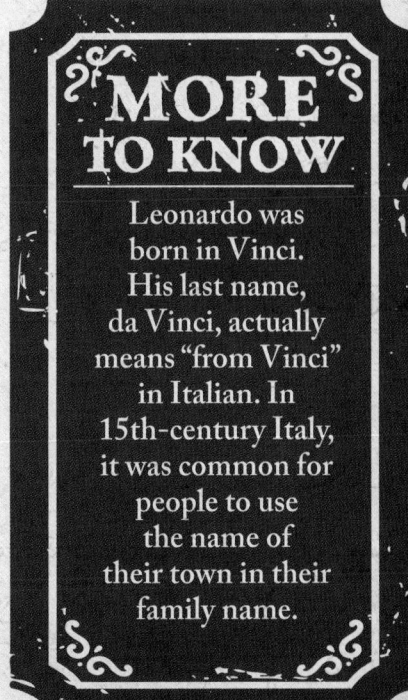

MORE TO KNOW

Leonardo was born in Vinci. His last name, da Vinci, actually means "from Vinci" in Italian. In 15th-century Italy, it was common for people to use the name of their town in their family name.

APPRENTICESHIP

As a teenager, Leonardo became an **apprentice** to Andrea del Verrocchio, an artist in Florence. Verrocchio was known for his beautiful sculptures. This was an important start to Leonardo's career. Under Verrocchio, he would learn that he had true talent, for *"many are they who have a taste and love for drawing, but no talent."*

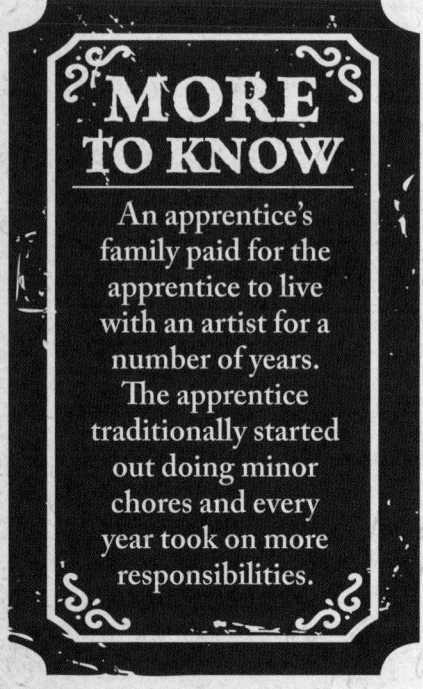

MORE TO KNOW

An apprentice's family paid for the apprentice to live with an artist for a number of years. The apprentice traditionally started out doing minor chores and every year took on more responsibilities.

Leonardo also learned about the tools of his trade. He made both paintbrushes and paints. He learned how to paint on a panel, or a flat piece of wood, and to create a fresco, which is a painting created on the damp plaster of a wall or ceiling.

Leonardo's earliest known drawing dates from a religious feast day in Florence in 1473. It's of the Arno valley and pays particular attention to landscape and plant details.

Leonardo da Vinci's earliest known work

It's thought that Leonardo da Vinci painted the angel on the left in Verrocchio's *Baptism of Christ.*

During the Renaissance, paintings were often completed by a group of artists directed by a master painter. Leonardo's first known contribution to such a work was an angel in Verrocchio's *Baptism of Christ.* Soon after, Verrocchio retired as a painter and focused on sculpting. Near the end of his life, he was commissioned to create a statue of famous soldier Bartolomeo Colleoni on horseback, one of his most celebrated works.

PAINTING

GUILDS

Only artists who had apprenticed to a master could join a guild. Guilds were organizations of skilled workers, often made up of the rich and powerful in a city. At one time in Florence, only guild members could vote or hold political office. There were guilds for merchants, doctors, weavers, bankers, and other kinds of jobs. When Leonardo joined the artists' guild in Florence at the age of 20, he was considered a master.

Around 1470, Leonardo finished his first painting, called *The Annunciation*. Like most paintings of the time, it had a religious subject. It showed the angel Gabriel appearing to Mary, the mother of Jesus. Critics still argue about whether Leonardo was responsible for the whole painting. Most agree he designed and sketched it.

Leonardo remained Verrocchio's assistant for about another 7 years. During that time,

Critics note how lifelike the angel Gabriel's wings are in The Annunciation. Leonardo's study of birds would have helped him create that effect.

he was accepted into the artists' guild of Florence. In 1477, he decided to strike out on his own.

In 1478, he wrote, *"I have begun the two Virgin Marys."* Experts believe that the *Benois Madonna* is one of them. Mary is shown with a happy, young face and is an example of Leonardo's early work. At that time, other artists' depictions, or representations, of Mary were stuffy and humorless.

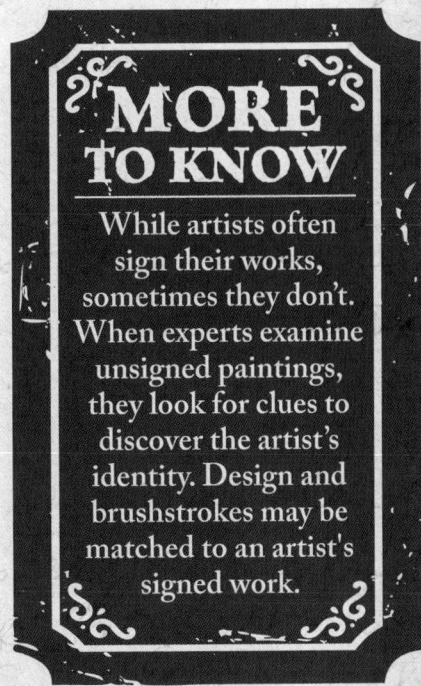

MORE TO KNOW

While artists often sign their works, sometimes they don't. When experts examine unsigned paintings, they look for clues to discover the artist's identity. Design and brushstrokes may be matched to an artist's signed work.

In the *Benois Madonna*, the baby Jesus reaches for a flower in Mary's hand.

When Leonardo was 30, he received a commission for *The Adoration of the Magi*. In the Bible, the Magi were the three wise men who came from the East to celebrate the birth of Jesus. Leonardo's depiction brought a fresh perspective to the scene. He gave lifelike emotion to the people surrounding the baby Jesus.

MORE TO KNOW

Saint Jerome in the Wilderness is another painting Leonardo started before leaving Florence. Like the *Adoration*, it was never finished.

Many artists painted people in religious paintings as calm and distant. Leonardo's vibrant faces were more entertaining.

Saint Jerome in the Wilderness

In the bottom right of *The Adoration of the Magi* is a young shepherd boy facing away from the crowd. He's believed by some to be a self-portrait of Leonardo. Also depicted are two knights fighting in the background. They possibly represent how the birth of Jesus was expected to defeat a violent, sinful past. Some art historians suggest that the figures who aren't featured with strong emotion reflect religious doubts that Leonardo was experiencing.

Leonardo wrote, *"A good painter has two subjects of primary importance: man and the state of man's mind. The first is easy, the second difficult, since it must be conveyed by means of the gestures and movements of the various parts of the body."* Though *The Adoration of the Magi* is considered a masterpiece, it was never finished. In 1482, Leonardo decided to leave Florence for the city of Milan.

THE MOVE
to Milan

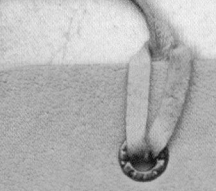

ON HIS OWN

Milan was much less artistically focused than Florence. Because there were fewer artists, Leonardo received more commissions. Though he had many friends, he believed he had to be alone to do his best work. He wrote in his notebooks that *"while you are alone you are entirely your [own] master and if you have one companion you are but half your own . . . And if you have many companions you will fall deeper into the same trouble."*

Leonardo presented his services to the ruler of Milan, Ludovico Sforza, as an entertainer. Leonardo was known for his beautiful singing voice and his skillful playing of the lyre, an instrument like a small harp. He also offered his services as an inventor of war machines, including one that could *"fling small stones"* and another that was like a modern tank.

When Leonardo first arrived, however, his first project was a painting: *The Virgin of the Rocks.* The rocks and caves in the background give a sense of another world. Mary, though older in age than in his previous

14

paintings, is still quite natural. Leonardo was beginning to study human **anatomy** at this time, which lent even more realism to his figures.

The original *The Virgin of the Rocks* (left) was created between 1483 and 1486. The second version (right) was created between 1506 and 1508.

Ludovico Sforza asked Leonardo to create a large horse statue in honor of his father. Leonardo worked on the bronze monument off and on for 12 years. At one point, he wrote: *"Again, the bronze horse may be taken in hand, which is to be to the immortal glory and eternal honour of the happy memory of the prince your father, and of the illustrious house of Sforza."* Sadly, he finally had to abandon it for good when the metal was needed to make weapons for war.

In 1495, Sforza hired Leonardo to paint a **mural** in a Florence **monastery**. The painting was *The Last Supper*, the famous depiction of Jesus and his followers sharing a meal before his death. The scene was 15 feet (4.6 m) by 29 feet (8.8 m) and took 2 years to complete.

Leonardo used paints that quickly flaked off the wall for *The Last Supper*. The work was restored several times over the years. Today, little of its original paint remains.

THE LAST SUPPER

The Last Supper was painted on the wall of the dining room in the Dominican monastery of Santa Maria delle Grazie. The scene was meant to appear as an extension of the room itself. All aspects of the painting lead the viewer to look at the figure of Jesus. Many painters, such as Rubens and Rembrandt, were influenced by Leonardo's composition, or the placement of the elements in his work.

LEONARDO'S *Notebooks*

SECRET SEA MACHINES

Leonardo also wrote about inventions similar to modern submarines and underwater breathing machines, but not in great detail. He worried they would be used for war: *"How and why I do not describe my method of remaining under water . . . I do not publish nor **divulge** these by reason of the evil nature of men who would use them as means of destruction at the bottom of the sea."*

In the mid-1480s, Leonardo began writing his thoughts down in notebooks. He planned on publishing books on the artistic and the scientific, including the study of plants, anatomy, painting, astronomy, and architecture. The notebooks are the best way to learn about who Leonardo was as an artist and a man.

Leonardo wrote a lot about flying. He studied birds and bats and was convinced that humans could learn to fly with the invention of a machine with wings: *"Remember that your flying machine must imitate no other than the bat, because the web is what by its union gives the armour, or strength to the wings."* He wrote this hundreds of years before the airplane was invented. Many of Leonardo's ideas were advanced for his time and, because of this, seemed impossible.

MORE TO KNOW

Leonardo kept small pads of paper in his belt so he'd always be ready to write down his thoughts.

A sketch from Leonardo's notebooks displays his idea for a flying machine based on a bat's wing.

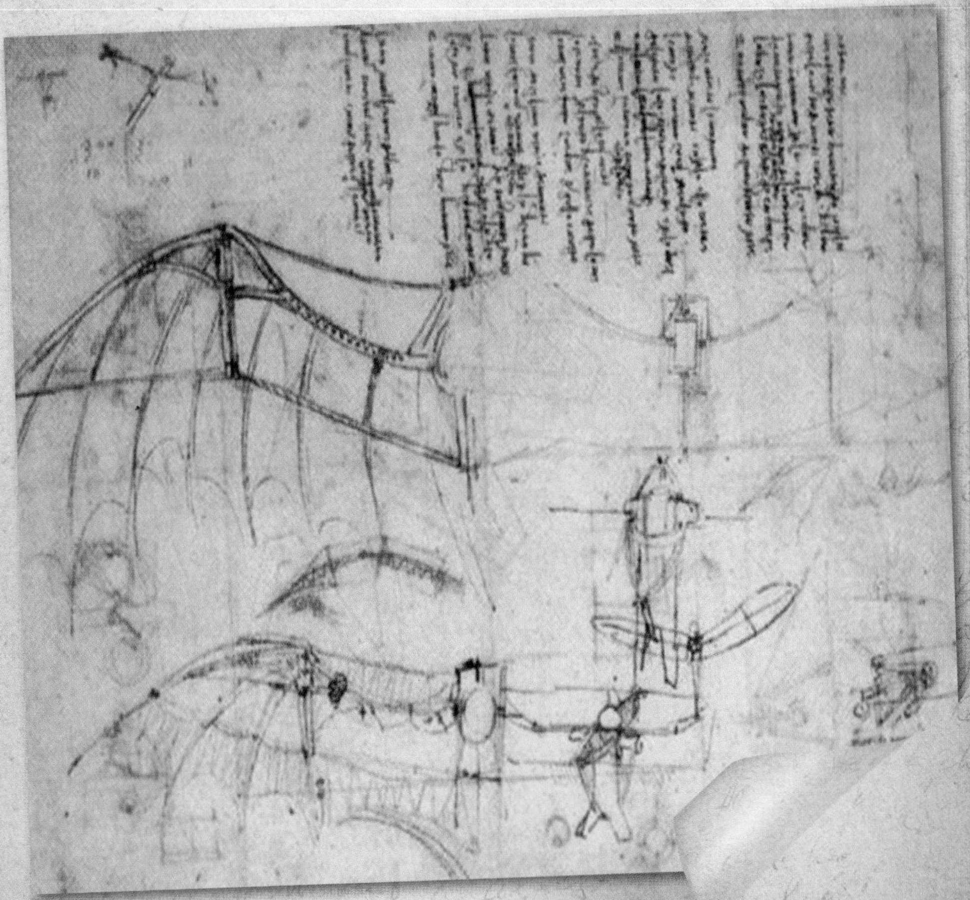

The MONA LISA

In 1499, Milan was invaded by France, and Ludovico Sforza fell from power. Leonardo left Milan after living there for 17 years. He traveled all over Italy. In 1502, he became a military engineer for the pope's army. He mapped cities and thought of ways to defend them from attack.

By 1503, Leonardo returned to Florence and began his most famous painting: the *Mona Lisa*. He worked on it for 3 years and even took it with him when he traveled. He didn't believe in hurrying to complete his artwork: *"It is well that you should often leave off work and take a little relaxation, because, when you come back to it you are a better judge; for sitting too close at work may greatly deceive you."*

MORE TO KNOW

The *Mona Lisa* has another title: *La Gioconda*.

The slight smile of the woman in the *Mona Lisa* and her direct stare at the viewer have fascinated art lovers for centuries. ⟶

THE MONA LISA

The *Mona Lisa* is one of the most popular paintings in history. It's said that the harmony between the smiling woman and the natural background reflects Leonardo's belief in the harmony between humanity and nature. Some experts believe the subject of the painting is a female version of Leonardo himself. Others think she was Lisa del Giocondo, the wife of a Florentine merchant. The *Mona Lisa* is on display in the Louvre Museum in Paris, France.

The SCIENTIST

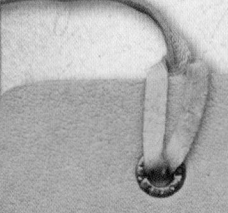

ARGUING OVER INHERITANCE

When Leonardo's father died in 1504 without a will, Leonardo's half brothers took all the inheritance. Leonardo had no right to it since his father and mother had never married. However, when his uncle Francesco died in 1507, he left an inheritance to Leonardo in his will. Leonardo's half brothers tried to take this money, too, so Leonardo took them to court. After several months, Leonardo won the case.

Leonardo first studied anatomy—especially the skeleton and muscles—to perfect his depictions of the human body. He wrote: *"It is indispensable to a Painter who would be thoroughly familiar with the limbs in all the positions and actions of which they are capable, in the nude, to know the anatomy of the **sinews**, bones, muscles, and tendons so that, in their various movements and **exertions**, he may know which nerve or muscle is the cause of each movement."*

Leonardo became fascinated by the entire body. He dissected, or took apart, bodies of different ages. He studied how blood flowed. He noted that some bodies had thicker blood vessels that would prevent a healthy amount of blood from passing through. We now know that this causes heart attacks.

Leonardo filled his notebooks with drawings of human muscles. He wrote: "Man has been called by the ancients a lesser world, and indeed the name is well applied."

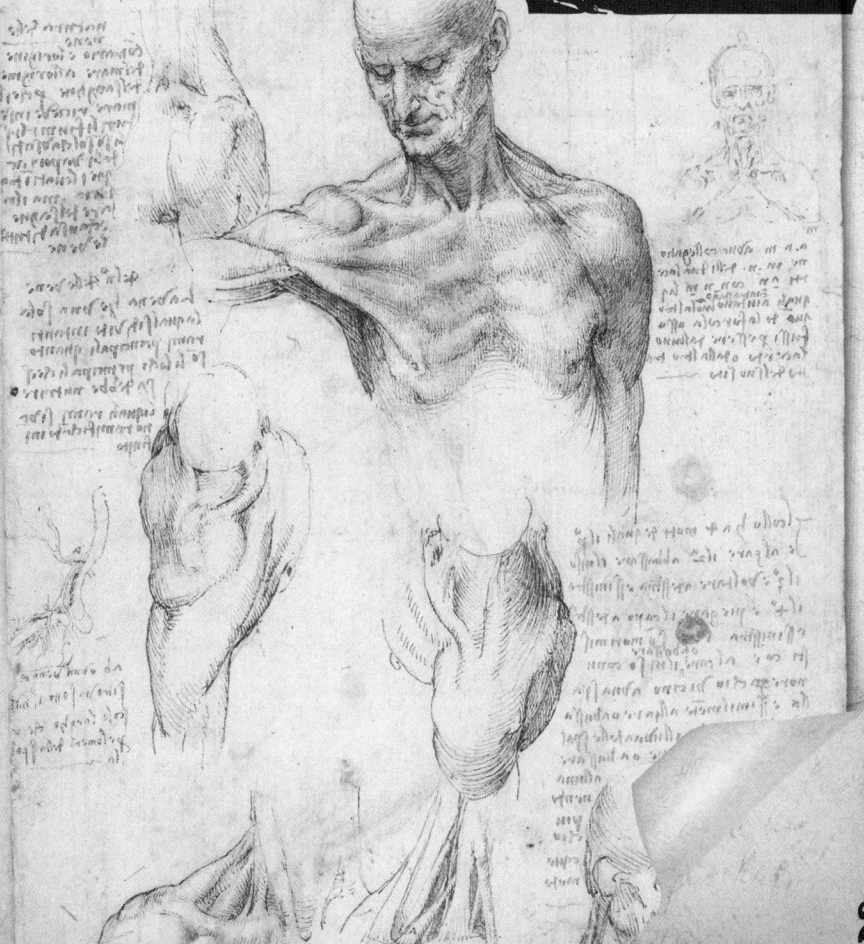

ROME
and France

In 1513, Leonardo moved to Rome when he was about 60 years old. He spent 3 years there. During this time, he studied mirrors. He used them for his artwork: *"I say that when you paint you should have a flat mirror and often look at your work as reflected in it, when you will see it reversed, and it will appear to you like some other painter's work, so you will be better able to judge of its faults than in any other way."* Leonardo also used mirrors in plans for an invention that could focus the sun's rays to boil water.

In 1516, Leonardo moved to France. There, he was named the *"First painter, architect, and engineer to the King."*

In the painting *St. John the Baptist*, Leonardo shows John coming out of the darkness. The light reflects the man's goodness.

ST. JOHN THE BAPTIST

St. John the Baptist is one of Leonardo's lesser-known works and probably his last. The oil painting was completed sometime around 1516. Some critics complain that Leonardo copied his own work, the *Mona Lisa*, in creating Saint John's smile. Leonardo was never afraid of criticism. He wrote, *"Certainly while a man is painting he ought not to shrink from hearing every opinion."*

25

LEONARDO'S *Death*

MIRROR WRITING

When writing in his notebooks, Leonardo da Vinci used mirror writing. This means he wrote his words from right to left and his letters backward. Pages can be read most easily when reading their reflection in a mirror. Though some think he did this as a kind of code to keep his writing secret, others think it was an unusual result of being left-handed. In any case, Leonardo wrote his notebooks to a reader, suggesting he hoped they would be published.

Leonardo da Vinci wasn't afraid of growing old. He wrote in a notebook: *"Men are in error when they lament the flight of time, accusing it of being too swift, and not perceiving that it is sufficient as it passes."*

He died in France on May 2, 1519, at the age of 67. An early account of his life reported he died in the arms of the French king, Francis I. However, it's generally believed that never happened.

Leonardo had made a will shortly before his death, leaving his many notebooks and artworks to Francesco Melzi, his student and secretary. Leonardo was buried in a church that was later destroyed during the French Revolution (1789–1799). The location of his grave is no longer known.

MORE TO KNOW

Leonardo's last work wasn't a painting, but a series of sketches called *Visions of the End of the World*. These are thought to illustrate the relationship between creation and destruction in nature.

This is a 19th-century painting by Jean Auguste Dominique Ingres called *The Death of Leonardo da Vinci*. King Francis I holds Leonardo as he draws his last breath.

LEONARDO'S *Legacy*

MORE TO KNOW

Leonardo's notebooks have been organized into collections. Each collection is called a codex.

Leonardo da Vinci is considered one of the greatest artists in history. However, his notebooks support his standing as a great scientist, too. He described the workings of the telescope 100 years before it was invented. He wrote about the movement of blood through the body before circulation was documented. He even considered gravity almost 200 years before Isaac Newton did. And since only 32 of his 40 notebooks have been located, there's still a lot we don't know about Leonardo's genius.

The Renaissance man wrote, *"What is fair in men, passes away, but not so in art."* It has been almost 500 years since his death, but Leonardo lives on through both his words and art.

This is a statue of Leonardo da Vinci at Piazza della Scala in Milan, Italy.

TIMELINE
LEONARDO'S LIFE

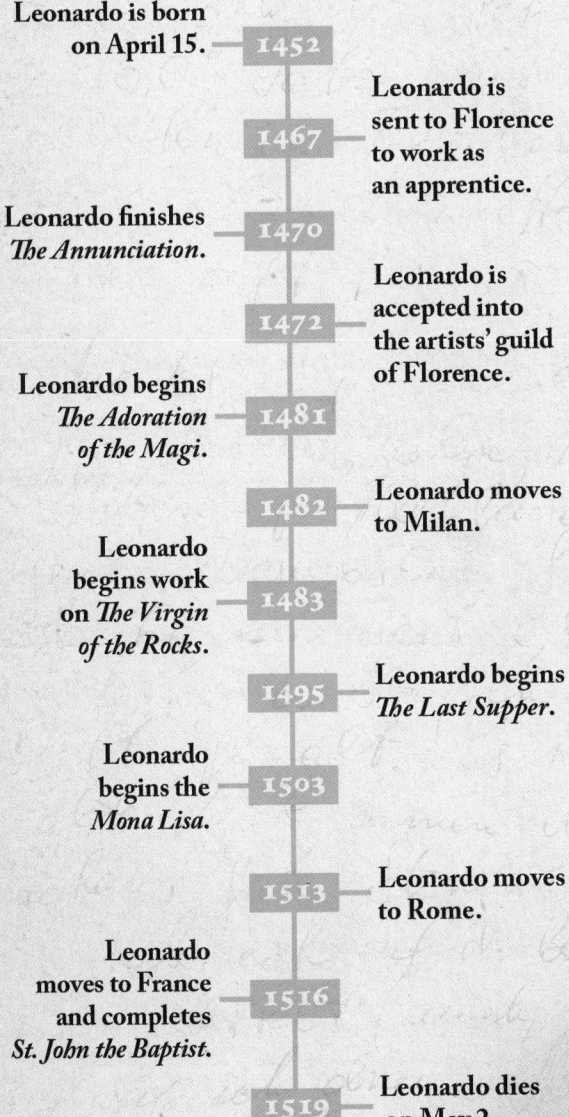

Leonardo is born on April 15. — **1452**

1467 — Leonardo is sent to Florence to work as an apprentice.

Leonardo finishes *The Annunciation*. — **1470**

1472 — Leonardo is accepted into the artists' guild of Florence.

Leonardo begins *The Adoration of the Magi*. — **1481**

1482 — Leonardo moves to Milan.

Leonardo begins work on *The Virgin of the Rocks*. — **1483**

1495 — Leonardo begins *The Last Supper*.

Leonardo begins the *Mona Lisa*. — **1503**

1513 — Leonardo moves to Rome.

Leonardo moves to France and completes *St. John the Baptist*. — **1516**

1519 — Leonardo dies on May 2.

UNFINISHED PAINTINGS

Leonardo left many paintings unfinished for practical reasons, such as a lack of resources or a move to a different location. However, he also left many works unfinished for no obvious reason. This may have been because he was interested in so many different topics that he got bored with projects easily. Some experts say that he was more interested in the way to approach a work—the process of creating—than in finishing it.

GLOSSARY

anatomy: a branch of science that studies the human body

apprentice: someone who learns a trade by working with a skilled person of that trade

architect: one who designs buildings

divulge: to make information known

exertion: physical effort

lament: to express unhappiness about something

monastery: a place where monks live and work together

mural: a large picture painted onto a wall

notary: a person with legal training who can perform certain actions under the law

prejudice: a feeling of dislike for a person or group because of race or other features

relish: to enjoy

rudder: a blade that helps steer a boat

sinew: strong tissue that connects muscle to bone

FOR MORE
Information

Books

Anderson, Maxine. *Amazing Leonardo da Vinci Inventions You Can Build Yourself*. Norwich, VT: Nomad Press, 2006.

Hall, M. C. *Leonardo da Vinci*. Edina, MN: ABDO Publishing, 2008.

Venezia, Mike. *Leonardo da Vinci*. New York, NY: Children's Press, 2015.

Websites

Leonardo da Vinci: Renaissance Man
legacy.mos.org/leonardo/bio.html
This short biography of Leonardo da Vinci includes information on his accomplishments in art, invention, and science.

Leonardo da Vinci 1452–1519
bbc.co.uk/science/leonardo/
Check out a photo gallery of Leonardo's paintings and an interactive 15th-century workshop.

INDEX